Better Than Yesterday

A GUIDE TO BECOMING THE BEST YOU

Keishaun Williams

Better Than Yesterday
A Guide To Becoming The Best You
by Keishaun Williams

Published by:
exploreSkillz Educational Publishing
Washington, DC 20003
www.exploreSkillzBooks.com

ISBN 978-0-578-82776-6

FIRST EDITION: December 2020
10 9 8 7 6 5 4 3 2 1

The Better Than Yesterday book is available at quantity discounts when utilized to promote products or services.

Author's Note

I never thought that one day I would write a book, but as God spoke to me, I listened. As he handed down his instructions, I knew I had to obey. It was an extraordinary feeling, a moment so indescribable that I believe everyone must experience on their own, to truly understand. It became clear to me what needed to be accomplished, but I knew the road ahead would not be easy. While the journey was quite difficult, I did have some help along the way from family, friends, and the good Lord above.

As a child, like many, I grew up in the church. However, I never fully understood why the congregation was always so joyful about Christ until I went through my own storm. But as God began to work through me, so did the Devil.

Better than Yesterday is a series of excerpts that aims to touch the hearts, minds, and souls of those who may be going through their individual storm. It is a series of self-reflection and a reminder that you will never be perfect, but there are ways that you can better yourself each and every day. With this book, I share my steps to a better tomorrow through short stories, personal experiences, and valuable life lessons. Better than Yesterday intends to help people become good human beings while transforming into the best possible versions of themselves.

This book is dedicated to my late nana, Mother Delphine Moore, who gracefully departed this Earth to be with the Lord on August 21, 2020. Nana always referred to me as her "hero", but in reality, she was mine. She was one of the few people who I could talk to about anything. She believed in me even when nobody else did. She was a great listener and one of the few people who could grasp my intuitive mind and way of thinking. Nana was sweet, kind, and loving to all she encountered. She was a God-fearing, Christian woman, and a prime example of how to live life the right way. Nana was an inspiration to us all, and she often expressed how she admired my unique writing ability. Before she passed, a few of her last words to me were, "You deserve to be understood." Through this book, I hope to accomplish just that and to allow my thoughts to resonate with readers around the world.

Special thanks to those who were a pivotal part in the production including my uncle, Keith Moore, and Ms. Gwen Knight, a forever friend of the family and Nana's #1 travel companion.

Introduction

I am not perfect, and I never will be. I know that I'm a good person, but I always seem to end up in bad situations. It's almost as if every time I take one step forward, I take two steps back. What is it that I'm doing wrong? Why can't I get it right? Truth is, I will never be perfect, and that's okay. I have come to accept that mistakes will always be a part of who I am, but they will never define who I am. And I haven't always made the right choices, but I won't let that discourage me from reaching my goals and dreams.

You see, we will all make mistakes during our lives, so why do we beat ourselves up when we do? Why are we so critical of our faults and missteps when they are inevitable? While we cannot avoid making mistakes, one thing we can do is learn from them. With every mistake comes opportunity; an opportunity to mature and develop into better versions of ourselves. So whatever your current perception of perfection is, throw it out the window – it doesn't exist. You will make mistakes and there will be times when you fall short. But don't let that deter you from reaching your destination. Don't let the constant battles of life break you down. Rise above your circumstances and commit to a lifestyle of continuous improvement so that you may become a role model for yourself and others. My friends, we will never be perfect, and that's okay. But even though we cannot eliminate our mistakes, we can choose to be better than yesterday.

About the Author

Keishaun Williams is a Master's student at West Virginia University. His major field of study is Sport Management, and he is scheduled to graduate in the Spring of 2021.

Keishaun is a man who has experienced his share of mistakes and hopes to help and guide others so that they might avoid some of the pitfalls he faced. He uses past experiences, encounters, and lessons learned in life to signify his spiritual identity through this book. Keishaun is self-driven and motivates himself to complete whatever task he sets his mind to.

He is a lover of life and has made it a priority to maintain a positive attitude, regardless of any situation in which he finds himself. Knowing he is blessed keeps him well balanced. While not perfect, Keishaun's heart is pure and filled with love for all humanity. Hopefully, one day, like many others before him, he will make a positive difference in this world.

His goal is to become a General Manager in the WNBA. His plan is to utilize his skills, experiences, and training to elevate the quality of performance of players as well as foster an inclusive, collaborative, and connected team environment.

Some of Keishaun's passions include, but are not limited to, spending time with friends and family, sports, staying fit, and food.

His desire is for people to recognize and respect him simply as a "good" man committed to a positive difference in the lives of others.

Contents

Adopt And Maintain A Healthy Lifestyle

To maintain a healthy lifestyle, one does not necessarily have to obtain a gym membership or drastically alter their diet. There are many ways to implement healthy habits into your daily life, not always requiring physical activity. Now I'm not saying that physical activity and exercise aren't important – because they are; however, it is not the only way that you can achieve an adequate level of health and well-being. Ultimately, one must find a sufficient balance to sustain and satisfy their overall physical and mental health to attain a healthful lifestyle.

To begin, practicing good hygiene is the first step in obtaining good health and promoting other healthy behaviors. By maintaining healthy hygiene habits, you can greatly diminish the possibility of the spread of illness and infections throughout the body. These actions can be extremely beneficial to you and others, especially with the current health pandemic that we are all experiencing. Furthermore, maintaining your physical appearance and becoming well-groomed is another way to engage in healthy lifestyle habits.

Now no one is expecting a massive makeover, or for you to completely ditch your current wardrobe. But, I will say that when you fully begin to manage and take care of your outward and physical appearances, your confidence and comfort within yourself will substantially skyrocket. I'm sure you're familiar with the phrase, "Look good, feel good," and that is all to be true. Consistently feeling good will encourage other areas of your life to grow and flourish, but only if you choose to commit.

In addition to maintaining your external image, you must regulate what you choose to put into your body as well. These choices may not just influence how you feel today, but they can have lasting effects that can be damaging to your long-term health. To reiterate, nobody is anticipating you to drastically alter your diet and I certainly am not here to supplement a diet plan. However, you must understand that the little choices make a big difference, particularly when it comes to food consumption. For example, if you're like me, you may have a sweet tooth that seems to never go away. But, that does not mean that I'm constantly pleasuring my sweet tooth, because that would be too detrimental to my current and future health. Plus, I have a considerably long family history of diabetes so I would only be setting myself up for failure. With that said, while I wish I could regularly satisfy my cravings, it becomes impossible if I want to uphold a lifestyle of healthy living. On the other hand, a continuous cycle of poor eating habits and nutritional neglect are sure to negatively impact the quality of your life. You'll start to realize that your energy will drain, and your focus and productivity may begin to dwindle. On top of that, your body will undeniably become more susceptible to certain chronic diseases such as diabetes, stroke, and cancer. So, do yourself and your future self a favor by implementing healthy habits into your daily routine today. The sooner you start, the better off you'll be.

In addition to diet, make sure to get plenty of sleep! I know it may not seem that important to you now, but I promise it will make a difference in the long haul. Getting the right amount of sleep, which has been studied to be at least 7 hours each night, can vastly improve, as well as preserve vital cognitive functions such as concentration and memory. This may be more difficult for some because of the differing circumstances of life, and I understand. However, sleep is indeed an essential component of our functionality and you may start to suffer if you frequently fail to meet your recommended sleep requirements.

All in all, there are countless ways to adopt and maintain a healthy lifestyle. The benefits are endless, whereas unhealthy habits slowly stimulate self-destruction. Don't wait until tomorrow or the next day to take control of your health; start now! And remember, it's the little choices that make a big difference.

Become Your Own Best Friend

People and relationships come and go. Throughout your life, you will cross paths with many different types of people, some permanent and some temporary. There are those you will build and foster meaningful relationships and those who will merely serve a specific purpose for the time being. Whatever the circumstance, you must remind yourself that none of these people will be with you forever. Only you can occupy that position.

Sure, people will come and go in and out of your life, but you can always count on you. But what does it exactly mean to become your own best friend? Well,

I'm glad you asked! I want you to think about one of your closest friends. Take a moment to reflect on that relationship including how you communicate, and the mutual level of love and respect that you share. The way you act towards your best, closest friend, is how you should towards yourself, because at the end of the day, you are somebody, too. Becoming your own best friend can grant you the confidence and courage to accept and appreciate who you truly are as an individual, regardless of what others may say or think about you. It will allow you to engage in more self-reflection and less self-criticism.

Mistakes will be an enduring part of your life. For example, when your best friend makes a mistake, I'm sure you don't belittle them or make them feel like any less of a person. Yet, whenever you make a mistake, you are quick to criticize and chastise yourself for a simple error that most likely can be corrected. I, too, am guilty of this, as I am my own worst critic. This can be a blessing and a curse. My point is, you wouldn't treat your best friend the same way you'd treat yourself for making an error or mistake. So be kind to yourself just as you would towards a close companion. Furthermore, becoming your own best friend is highly beneficial in times of loneliness and isolation which we will all experience during our lives. Loneliness can be extremely difficult to endure. However, the good news is that you are never alone no matter how you may feel at a particular point.

I've actually had a lot of experience with this as a kid. I was heavily misunderstood, primarily by my parents. We rarely saw eye to eye on certain situations and I never really could go and talk to them about my thoughts and feelings. We never talked about drugs, alcohol, or mental health. We didn't talk about the birds and the bees or other common conversations expected from our parents. Physically, they were present, but emotionally they were absent. As a result, I would isolate myself the majority of the time and bottle up my feelings and emotions. Now, I'm not saying that this was a healthy coping mechanism, but it did teach me some things. Mainly, it taught me how to appreciate being alone and how to become comfortable in my own company. I laughed and I cried with myself. I spent a lot of time getting to know Keishaun. And you know what I discovered? He was a pretty cool guy. I learned to cherish myself because, at the end of the day, I was all that I had. While these times were tough, I got a chance to meet one of my best friends in the whole world – me!

Another instance where I had to put these principles into practice was as a graduate student at West Virginia University. I enrolled in their sport management program after completing my undergraduate degree at Radford University in Virginia in 2019. During my undergrad years, I was widely-known throughout campus by peers, faculty, and other employees. Now I'm not one to toot my own horn, but I was that dude. You couldn't catch me on campus without walking or chopping it up with somebody. But when I came to West Virginia, it was a completely different story. I didn't know a soul and nobody knew me. I was alone. From my very first day in Morgantown, I knew I had to figure something out. But this time, I wasn't there to make friends. My goal was to create connections that would benefit me in jumpstarting my career in the sports industry (although I did finally make a few friends). Even so, since the program's course material was hardly too challenging or time-consuming, I had quite a bit of down time on my hands. I had no other choice but to get in tune with myself and figure out how I was going to stay sane for the short time I was here. It wasn't easy at first, but the more I began to enjoy my own company in this unfamiliar territory, the smoother it became. I was my own best friend and our relationship was pretty incredible; and still is, to this day.

When you are your own best friend, you are encouraged to become more self-reliant, which can be beneficial to you in the many trying times of life. Being alone won't be as dreadful, because you are never alone. While relationships are a fundamental and essential part of our lives, there is nothing more important than the relationship you form with yourself. Becoming your own best friend will help you to navigate life through the difficult times while providing an eternal companion you may have never known you had.

Control Your Thoughts

In order to fully develop and progress into the best version of yourself, you must first command your way of thinking. Your life is a reflection of your thoughts, so it's paramount that you keep them positive and not let them discourage or derail you. As my mother would always say, "Your thoughts control your attitude, your attitude controls your actions, and your actions control your destiny!" Sometimes it can be super challenging to maintain a positive attitude and a bright outlook on life, especially when it seems like nothing is going your way and your world is slowly falling apart. I, too, experience similar feelings of doubt and hopelessness, but I do not let these temporary emotions to take control of who I am.

Certain circumstances can make it difficult to sustain positive thoughts, but one must conclusively shift their way of thinking to see a substantial change in their life. Controlling your thoughts require practice and patience as does anything else you want to master. Your thoughts can be tough to manage and more times than not, what we speculate about on a daily basis are things that are out of our control or haven't even happened. Everything begins and ends in the mind so you must take over the reins and dictate your journey. If you let your thoughts run wild, they will begin to run your life. After all, your thoughts control your attitude, your attitude controls your actions, and your actions control your destiny.

When a person fails to control their thoughts, they fail to control their life. Our various thoughts and thought processes are directly related to how we interact and engage with different people, places, and things. If you are to think negatively about a particular person or situation, odds are you are going to display negative behaviors towards them. Our attitudes are a direct showcase of our thoughts, which, in turn, are represented through our actions.

So, the only way to consistently exhibit positive attitudes and actions is to internalize positive thoughts. It is your actions that will influence the events that will happen in your life and determine how successful or unsuccessful you will ultimately be. Remember, you are in control, but it all begins and ends in the mind. Control your thoughts so that you may control your destiny!

Count Your Blessings

Let's face it - life can be hard at times. Like really, really hard. I've been beaten, bruised, and knocked down. Sometimes, I just feel like dropping everything and giving up. But that would be too easy. Yes – life is hard, and at times it feels as if the entire universe is against me. Even so, I am blessed!

I know that whatever pain and difficulties I may be dealing with, there is somebody out there facing far more issues. Therefore, I cannot complain. Despite my trials and tribulations, I am forever grateful. I'm grateful because my past has not defined my future. I'm grateful because, despite what I've done, God had not stopped watching over me even at times when I wasn't deserving of his grace and mercy. To be truthful, I should either be dead or in jail but God had different plans. I'm lucky to be where I am today and because of that, I cannot complain.

I want to shine some light on the phrase "Count Your Blessings" for a bit because I believe it to be of the utmost importance and extremely beneficial in life. It also happens to be one of my best mottos to live by because it is so powerful and truly mind-altering. Shoot, I love it so much that I even decided to get the words "Count Your Blessings" tattooed across my chest. But in all seriousness, the first step to a better life is to count your blessings. You may not be where you want to be, but hey, at least you're not where you used to be. You may not have it all, but at least you have something. And though you may not realize it at times, you have so much to be thankful for! We all know how easy it can be to get caught up in focusing on all of the negative events that have occurred throughout our lives. But instead of fixating on all that went wrong or what could've been, let's shift our focus to all that has gone well, particularly when things potentially could have gone either way. You'll see that once you shift into a mindset of consistent positive thinking, nothing can stop you.

Expressing gratitude for the endless gifts of life can reap tremendous benefits for your physical and mental health. However, expressing gratitude can be exceedingly more difficult for some than others for several reasons. And I get that. It's not easy to express gratitude when you are accustomed to adversity. It's not easy to show appreciation for the good things in life when you're dying on the inside. It's not easy but it is possible.

If you're someone who finds trouble expressing gratitude, try familiarizing yourself with the Three Blessings Exercise, as this can be an exceptional aid. The Three Blessings Exercise was introduced by Dr. Martin Seligman, an American psychologist, author, and educator. He is also commonly referred to as the

"Father of Positive Psychology." Positive psychology is an exceptional concept that aims to allow individuals to maximize their overall life quality and satisfaction by identifying and evaluating the pleasant events and experiences that they've encountered. The purpose of this exercise is to help those build and maintain feelings of appreciation for the many blessings bestowed upon them on a daily basis.

To complete the exercise, follow these instructions: At the end of each day before you go to sleep, take a few moments to think about three things that went well during the day and why they went well. That's it! You can choose to document these moments or simply visualize them. But understand that these events don't have to be anything extraordinary. The purpose of this exercise is to highlight positive experiences no matter the magnitude. For example, you may have had a delicious meal earlier in the day or perhaps you talked with an old friend. Whatever the case, just take some time to show a moment of appreciation for that experience, how it made you feel, and anything else that made it a pleasant encounter. That's all. And the more you practice, the easier it will become for you to focus on your blessings rather than your burdens.

If you still have trouble expressing gratitude for the good things in life, think about this: You're surviving in what arguably is the worst global pandemic this world has ever seen. Let me give you a few facts and figures just to put things into perspective. As of this day, there have been almost ten million American's who have contracted the COVID-19 disease and nearly fifty million worldwide in 2020. Additionally, the death toll has surpassed 200,000 American's and 1.2 million people across the globe. I want you to think about that for a second – 200,000 American's, 1.2 million people. Unfortunately, that number will most likely be substantially higher by the time you're reading this. So, I want you to become aware of how blessed you truly are and not just as it pertains to this deadly disease. People are being taken away from this Earth in large numbers. Young, old, healthy, sick, it doesn't matter. My friends, death is real and it is very random. Don't waste your time dwelling on your downfalls. Learn to appreciate the good things in life no matter how big or how small. You're far more fortunate than many so it is crucial that you continuously remind yourself of that fact, especially when you start to take things for granted. Above all, you are alive! Despite what could've been, God had other plans for you. So count your blessings, not your burdens, and the beauty of life shall reveal itself unto you.

Distance Yourself From Negativity

Who and what you choose to surround yourself with can have a much stronger influence on you than what you may think. Typically, your environment plays a pivotal role in directing and shaping one's way of thinking and our actions and behaviors. As a result, it becomes critical to your overall well-being when deciding who and what you wish to engage and surround yourself with daily. Yet, how can someone identify if they are undoubtedly amongst negativity? You will know you're in the midst of negativity the moment you begin to question if you are. You might start to feel uneasy in that particular situation or even stressed. That is the main indicator. You'll know for certain if you're in the company of negativity if the encounters start to make you feel stressed, anxious, or uncomfortable.

It might be difficult for you to recognize at first, but once you begin to distance yourself, everything becomes evident. But I know this is easier said than done. There are several factors that can make it difficult for a person to separate themselves from negativity. Yet, probably the biggest reason why it's so tough for many of us to move on from a negative person or situation is because of the physical or emotional attachments we have made with them. And I understand. Once you've established a strong connection with someone or something, it almost seems as if they can do no wrong. Our feelings can blind us from the truth and make it challenging to discontinue a relationship regardless of the amount of warning signs. We all have experienced these types of dilemmas at one point with a friend, a partner, or perhaps a family member. But you must remember to prioritize your own health and happiness and if that involves cutting ties, then so be it.

Distancing yourself from negativity also includes bad habits, practices, and tendencies. For example, like many people, you might have a bad smoking or drinking habit. You like how it makes you feel in the moment – but depending on the frequency and regularity of this particular activity, the harmful long-term effects can potentially outweigh the short-term benefits. If you feel somewhat triggered, maybe it's time to distance yourself. Now I'm not here to tell you it's going to be easy, but it is going to be worth it. As for myself, I had to learn how to distance myself from activities that weren't helping me become a better man. In particular, I loved to go out and party – still do. Now, just to be clear, there's nothing wrong with going out and having a good time. But more often than not, I would go out and have entirely too good of a time (or at least that's what I thought). You see, my main issue was that I lacked self-control in these types of situations. Like a lot of you, I typically would indulge in a few alcoholic beverages before stepping out. We call this the "pregame". So before I could even arrive at my destination, I was already feeling good and loose. Some of y'all know exactly what I'm talking about. But it didn't stop there. Once I arrived at the party, or the bar, or wherever it was, the "fun" always continued as well as the drinking and spending. And before I would know it, I'd be waking up the next day, fully-clothed, in my bed, wondering what happened and how I got there. This destructive cycle lasted for quite a while until one day I finally realized that I needed to make a drastic change. I was tired of waking up clueless and not being able to remember all the "fun" I had the night before. I was tired of being cautious about checking my bank account the following morning. I know I'm preaching to somebody right now! But in order to truly elevate my life, I knew I had to separate myself from that scene for a bit.

Again, there's absolutely nothing wrong with going out, indulging in a few adult beverages (if you're of age, of course), and having a good time. But for me, the after effects heavily outweighed the benefits. My poor habits were not allowing me to reach my full potential so I decided to take some time away. Now it wasn't easy, mainly because I had become so accustomed to this lifestyle and toxic behavior. But it needed to be done. If I wanted to evolve into the man I knew I was capable of becoming, I had to distance myself.

Once I did, that's when the true transformation started to take place. Instead of going out and getting hammered each night, I used that time to become a better Keishaun. I began to engage myself in much healthier habits such as reading and writing. At first, I missed the party scene – a lot. But the more I distanced myself, the easier it became to adapt to this new lifestyle, and it felt good. I was gaining valuable insight on how to truly become a man from books I never would have considered reading. I began to use my time purposefully rather than to self-destruct. Additionally, my bank account was extremely thankful and before I knew it, I was slowly but surely becoming a man.

Don't get me wrong! I still love to go out, indulge, and have a good time. But for a brief period, I had to distance myself from that environment and the negative consequences that come with it. Once you begin to distance yourself, that is when the real growth begins. Distancing yourself from negativity is truly the first step in making a positive change in your life. Detachment from these particular things will allow you to grow as an individual while encouraging a new and improved set of behaviors and lifestyles. We might not ever be able to avoid negativity, but we can always choose whether or not to engage in it. Ultimately, these decisions will shape and influence who you are and what you may become. Distance yourself from negativity so that you can finally experience the transformation you've been craving!

Do Unto Others As You Would Have Them Do Unto You

I'm sure you're familiar with the Golden Rule. By adhering to this most basic ethical principle, you can increasingly enhance multiple aspects of your life while setting the standard for those around you. Despite what you may have heard or been taught, being a decent human being can actually take you a very long way in life. You should also be familiar with the phrase, "what goes around, comes around." I must say, I've experienced my fair share of good and bad karma to let you know that this is ever so true. I am not perfect so I can admit that I have hurt people in the past. But in return, I've experienced that same hurt. It may have not always been immediately after the fact, but believe me when I tell you, it all came back to me. Now I've also done right by a lot of people, whether it was helping them with something, giving them words of encouragement, or simply being a decent human being. That energy has always reciprocated back to me, as well. So yes, being a decent human being can take you a long way. My point is that you can't repeatedly do wrong by people and expect good things to happen for you in return. Of course, you are not perfect so you won't always make the right decisions, but you can at least try.

Effort goes a long way in this instance, too. We all know how hard life can be and sometimes that can make it challenging to consistently act in a principled, moral manner. Even so, you must not allow the unfavorable circumstances of life to break you down and ultimately affect how you act towards others. We are all going through something, but that doesn't mean we should let our situations alter our attitude and outlook on the world. No matter what, you can always be a decent human being. You can always choose to treat others with the same love, respect, and kindness that you desire. If you continue to do this, despite your circumstances, good things will eventually come your way. Furthermore, this consistent behavior becomes highly contagious and serves as a model for others in the community. When other people see that you're doing the right thing, they too will be inclined to do so. On the other hand, when you are deceitful and dishonest, others may believe that this behavior is acceptable and that they can also get away with this behavior. That's why it's always important to act in a virtuous manner especially when you're in the public eye. Your actions can influence many who may look up to you, including family members, friends, and peers. Therefore, do unto others so that you can serve as a positive role model in a remarkably discouraging society and implement change throughout the world.

Don't Let Anybody Have Control Of Your Happiness Because It Comes From Within

Oftentimes we tend to seek satisfaction from external sources such as money, material possessions, and other people (just to name a few). But one must understand that while these objects may provide temporary pleasure, lasting happiness will always come from within. Surely you won't achieve eternal satisfaction from the world no matter how long and far you search. So remember to stay true to yourself, because ultimately, that is where you will attain the greatest amount of gratification.

With that said, it does you no good to attempt to gain the approval of your peers because neither them or the front you've put on can satisfy your happiness. You are in control! When you are the sole commander of your happiness, it will seem as if nothing can stop you and you will soon realize that no person, situation, or circumstance could ever take that feeling away. No matter what may be going on in or around your life, you will remain comfortable and confident because you are in control. Additionally, the unfortunate events that you are bound to experience throughout your existence will not bother or upset you as much. We cannot escape these occurrences as they are a part of life.

Yet, when you allow these circumstances to disrupt your feelings and emotions, you relinquish the title of commander of your happiness and you are no longer in control. You may have heard the saying "those who anger you control you", but this isn't limited to just people. When certain situations can make you feel a similar way, they also control you. Let's take a look at a quick scenario: It's Friday, you're having a great day at work, and you finished all your assignments so you get to leave early to start the weekend. But on the ride home, you unexpectedly drive over a nail in the road causing a flat tire. Now you are faced with two options. You could either get extremely frustrated, throw a tantrum, and start shouting all types of obscenities or you can remain calm and understand that bad things will happen. That's the simple nature of life. Sure your tire is flat on what seemed to be the best day ever, but you won't allow that one fixable thing to take you out of your positive mindset.

Now that we've analyzed both options, which do you think would benefit you the most? Yes, bad things are going to happen but you cannot allow these events to influence or control you because they will surely snatch your joy. The same goes for people. Don't allow people to make you react in a way that is harmful to you because of their poor decisions. Remember, your happiness begins with you and it can only escape you if you let it. You are in control. The sooner you realize this, the better off you'll be.

Eliminate Self-Doubt

Self-doubt is defined as the lack of confidence in oneself and one's abilities. It is a mental prison in which we confine ourselves, that can direct the course of our lives if we let it. It is a mindset that greatly diminishes your confidence and feeds you constant lies that you are incapable and unqualified. Truth is, we all have our moments of self-doubt. But if it brings us no benefit, why do we allow ourselves to continue to feel this way time and time again?

There are several factors that can influence this feeling of self-doubt such as fear of failure, demoralizing dialogue, and constant comparisons. Even so, when these challenges present themselves, you must remind yourself that you are capable and that you can do anything in the world as long as you set your mind to it. I know that may sound cliché, but it's entirely true. Our fear of failure is probably the biggest influence on why we experience these emotions. I'm sure you've said to yourself at least once, "I don't know if I can do this," or "That task seems too difficult." I've been there, too. But if you let yourself believe that lie, you've already lost. You can't do it because, in your mind, you've already convinced yourself otherwise. I've seen many cases where this is far too common, where people won't try something simply because they don't want to fail at it. But what a lot of folks don't realize is that failure is okay. In fact, sometimes we need to fail in order to learn or find an alternative path. Now, I don't want to burst your bubble, but let me tell you that you won't succeed in everything you do in life. But you will come to realize that failure does not mean defeat. Failure only exists when you stop trying!

Second, demoralizing dialogue can be just as influential in activating self-doubt. Demoralizing dialogue can severely discourage you and crush your hopes and dreams. There has probably been a time in your life that you can vividly remember where someone has discouraged you with their words. Think about that moment and how it made you feel. Not so good, right? You can have all the confidence in the world regarding a specific goal or task and it takes just one person to say something negative that derails your entire determination and motivation. But just because someone tells you that you can't do something doesn't mean it's true. Only you know what you're capable of, so don't let the ignorant opinions of others throw you off your game.

But like others, you too can throw yourself off your game with your own dialogue. How you communicate with yourself is an essential part of believing in yourself and maximizing your full potential. Negative self-talk can make you doubt yourself in any situation, even if there isn't any legitimate reason to.

When this happens, make it a priority to doubt your doubts. Sometimes we can become our own worst enemy by letting the negative voices in our head guide our thoughts and decisions, all while hindering us from achieving our goals and ambitions. Truthfully, the voices in our heads can sometimes be the biggest haters and critics. When the voices in my head start telling me that I can't do something, I simply laugh it off. That's really all you can do sometimes! So, the next time you're contemplating doing something, and the little voices in your head start to tell you that you can't, laugh it off and say "watch me". You'd be surprised to find out what you're capable of achieving when you just try! Always remember to doubt your doubts. Don't let yourself throw you off your game.

Finally, the cycle of constant comparisons is another significant reason why we all experience self-doubt. Now I'm sure you've been compared to somebody else at least once in your life. If you have brothers or sisters, you can probably relate. To those readers, I'm almost certain you've heard this once upon a time – "Why can't you be more like your brother or sister?" And while that quick, tiny comparison may seem meaningless, it can actually take a tremendous toll on one's confidence and belief in their individual abilities. When you're constantly being compared to someone else, you worry that what you're doing isn't good enough, or more importantly, that you're not good enough. And that's where the self-doubt begins.

There are many factors that can trigger this destructive feeling. But in spite of this, you must overcome these obstacles and tell yourself that you are capable. You are determined. You can do this. When I first got the idea of writing this book, my self-doubt was through the roof. I had never written a book before so how would I know what to do, what to write? What if nobody likes it? What if it's a complete and utter failure? There goes that demoralizing dialogue that I was talking about earlier. But regardless of my fears and whatever tricks my mind was trying to play on me, I calmly reminded myself, "You can do this!" So I did. And you can, too. You can do anything if you put your mind to it. Not to say that writing this book was easy, because it wasn't. In fact, it was probably one of the most difficult things I've had to do in my life thus far. But I believed in myself. I knew I was capable. And that made all the difference.

To be clear, having doubts in dire circumstances is perfectly reasonable. However, you should consistently practice eliminating self-doubt so that you can elevate your confidence and enhance the overall quality of your life. So, stop holding yourself back. You can do anything you set your mind to and the only person stopping you is you!

Embrace Your Flaws

Everyone has imperfections which can make us unique in our own way. But let's keep it real. We all have at least one thing about ourselves that we wish we could change or improve. Maybe you wish that you were taller, or skinnier, or perhaps even more attractive. These are all very natural desires. But let me tell you, it does no good to wish to be something that you are not. The best thing you can do is simply be you. While we may be unhappy with specific traits or features, certain things, unfortunately, we just cannot change.

Whatever it may be, I want to reassure you that your insecurities are not nearly as dreadful as you perceive them to be. With that being said, why would you not love and embrace the skin you are in? Truth is, there will always be someone out there who is better than you. There will always be someone who is smarter, stronger, better looking, etc. But one thing is for sure, they can never be you. Learning to accept yourself for who you are, flaws and all, is the greatest way to achieve peace of mind and total serenity. Furthermore, you should learn to love and embrace your imperfections so that you can fully love yourself. Now just because you do this does not mean that you will never again experience feelings of self-consciousness or insecurity. In fact, we wouldn't be human if we didn't encounter these emotions every now and then. But just because you experience these feelings, that doesn't mean they have to take control of who you are.

Our insecurities can often make us feel isolated and detached from everyone and everything around us, which in turn damages our everyday and personal relationships. However, once you learn to embrace your flaws, you vastly reduce these toxic thoughts and acquire the necessary confidence to enjoy and experience life to the fullest.

The first step in embracing your flaws and welcoming confidence into your life is to acknowledge what it is that's bothering you. For instance, if you think you have a wide nose, acknowledge it instead of trying to cover it up with makeup and contour techniques. I promise you will feel much better about yourself! Acknowledging your flaws first helps you to understand any underlying causes for that concern and eventually allows you to be at peace with them. But that doesn't mean that you should become comfortable with all of your imperfections, particularly the ones you can change. For example, while you may not be able to alter a wide nose (without plastic surgery), you can alter poor procrastination habits. But just like any other flaw, in order to embrace, you must first acknowledge. In this case, acknowledging will help you to realize that a problem exists, and it will encourage you to make adjustments as needed.

One of my biggest personal flaws, perhaps, is probably the fact that I cannot stay serious even at times when I should. I don't know what it is or why it happens, but that's just how it's always been for me. I could be in the most serious of situations, but I'm still bound to let out a chuckle or at least crack a smile for no reason whatsoever. It usually happened whenever my parents would scold my siblings or me at the dinner table, which most of the time got us into more trouble. My mother would always turn to me and ask what was so funny, but I never could give her an answer. And that was the honest truth. Nothing was funny. But somehow, someway, I would still find a way to laugh for whatever reason. This had to be one of my greatest flaws growing up because it typically got me into trouble and I never could explain what was so funny. But after a while, I learned to accept that this was just a part of who I was. Sometimes, I'll crack a smile or a smirk for no apparent reason. Sometimes, I'm silly in serious situations and I can't seem to understand why. So one day, when my mother asked me what was so funny, I told her I didn't know and I just couldn't help it. While this response didn't necessarily win her or my father's favor, they both knew that it would be unfair to discipline me for something that I couldn't control. Besides, it wasn't like I had been disrespectful on purpose. I really couldn't help it.

Of course, this is something that I've had to work on over the years, but that doesn't mean I don't slip up sometimes. I know that in order to make it anywhere in this world, I'm going to have to be serious in certain situations. Therefore, I've learned to control my smirks, smiles, and giggles in those types of settings. But, again, I am not perfect and sometimes I slip up. And that's okay. That's just a part of who I am. So, ladies and gentlemen, learn to embrace your flaws but do not let them define you. Instead, use them as motivation for personal growth and development and for improvements on the imperfections that you can change. Above all, embrace what makes you, because there's no one else quite like you.

Forgive Those Who Have Done You Wrong

Forgiveness is defined as a conscious, deliberate decision to release feelings of resentment or vengeance toward a person or group who has harmed you. While forgiving others for their wrongdoings can be difficult, it is something that we must do in order to let go of past hurt and move forward with our lives. To begin, we should forgive others because God has first forgiven us. Despite our countless falls and shortcomings, God looked past our imperfections and has loved us unconditionally. None of us are perfect – in fact, we're far from it. We continuously do things that are displeasing to him, yet he always finds a way to forgive (if we truly repent). There are no limitations to God's forgiveness, no matter what sinful acts we've committed. So if God can forgive us for basically anything, why do we find it so difficult to forgive others when they perpetrate against us?

We should attempt to mirror him in this way so that we may heal our mind, body, and spirit and develop a forgiving heart. I know forgiveness can be tough, especially when those who have done you wrong don't deserve it. But let me tell you, the act of forgiveness isn't for them – it's for you. You must learn to forgive for yourself because you deserve inner peace. Even if what that person or group of people did to you was unimaginable, you must forgive them. Because once you begin to forgive others, you begin to free yourself.

You begin to free yourself from the hurt and pain. You begin to free yourself from the shackles that have imprisoned you mentally and physically as a result of the words and actions of other people. With forgiveness, you get to reclaim control of your life and command your future. But just because you forgive somebody for what they have done does not mean that you have to forget what they did to you. In fact, you shouldn't. You shouldn't forget the physical or emotional harm that was brought on by another person so that you can learn from these experiences and use them as future reference points.

However, just because you kept in mind what was did, does not mean that you should hold a grudge. Holding a grudge is actually one of the worst things you can do. Additionally, when you hold a grudge, it does not affect the perpetrator nearly as much as it affects you and your overall health. You may have heard the phrase "Holding a grudge is like drinking poison and expecting the other person to get sick." In other words, you're the only one that's affected by it! When you hold a grudge towards a particular person or group of people, you carry these feelings of anger and resentment that hinder your ability to grow, develop, and move forward from pain. Bearing these feelings can also negatively impact current and future relationships. Furthermore, dwelling on the past can make you bitter or hateful. When you hold a grudge, you subsequently give that person or persons a sense of power and control over your life. Or, as some would say, "Rent free." So, I advise you to let go of the pain. Let go of the grudge. If not for anything else, do it for the sake of your health.

Letting go of a grudge can also allow you to understand why someone hurt you in the past. While this does not excuse the hurt, forgiveness can help you find empathy and give you the opportunity to see things from their perspective. This still may not change how you feel about the person, but at least, it will provide you with an alternative point-of-view and perhaps some clarification as to why. But I do want to make one thing very clear – forgiveness and weakness are not synonymous! It takes a strong and willing person to forgive because it's much more difficult to let go of hurt and pain than to keep it.

I had to teach myself how to forgive an entire town in which I was raised. Ah, good ole, Jackson, New

Jersey. As a kid, I had always thought that I would eventually make it to play professionally in the NFL or NBA. Now, I am clear that this is a common dream for youngsters, but I firmly believed that I could do it. Because to this day, God has blessed me with a unique athletic ability that became clear at a very young age. And if you ask anybody who grew up with me, they'll tell you the same thing.

My entire life I dreamt of playing professional football or basketball. But I really favored football because that was my first love and I was significantly better at the sport. I started playing Pop Warner in Jackson at the age of 8 and from the first time I touched the field, I knew I had a gift – and people started to notice. I was faster, quicker, and smarter than my teammates. To be honest, I was just better than most of the kids my age. I even had a few coaches and parents say to me that one day I would make it to the NFL. My love and passion for the game only grew as I continued to make a name for myself in this youth football league. But unfortunately, my world flipped upside-down the moment I arrived at Jackson Memorial High School. Upon entering my freshman year, I had a vision. I was going to play football for four years, excel at it as usual, and eventually earn a scholarship to play at the next level. Boy, was I in for a rude awakening! As the season approached, the team became divided into three levels: freshmen, junior varsity, and varsity. I was on the freshman squad as a running back, but I wasn't the only one. There were about three other guys who played the same position, but in my mind, I was better than all of them. And truthfully, I was. However, as the season progressed, my love for the game dwindled – and fast. Every single game we played, we had a different starting running back and most of the time, it wasn't me. But when it was my time to shine, I did just that. Even so, it wasn't enough to gain the respect of my coaches to start me or even just give me a few extra touches. I became used to standing on the sideline, just watching. I became a bench-warmer which was something I had never experienced my entire life. Now, you're probably thinking to yourself, "Well, you probably just weren't that good." But that was far from the truth and everybody in town knew that. The primary reason why I wasn't getting the same treatment as the other boys, or respected as I should, was simply because of politics and the color of my skin. I wasn't the type of player to kiss up to the coaches or the one to sell the most candy for the fundraisers. I wasn't the player to associate myself with my teammates with who I shared absolutely nothing in common other than our love for the game. Those who are familiar with or grew up in Jackson, New Jersey, know exactly what I'm talking about. I'll simply put it like this: black athletes didn't stand a chance competing at the next level playing in this town! We surely were not awarded the same opportunities as our white counterparts. That's as clear as it gets.

Feeling undervalued and underappreciated, I decided to quit the team after my freshman year. That was one of the hardest decisions of my life because I loved the game of football so much and I was extremely gifted at it. But I was tired of being treated like shit. I was tired of being walked over. I was tired of watching from the sidelines even though I was better than whoever was on the field. I was sick and tired of being a benchwarmer.

After two years, I decided to return for my senior season because I just couldn't imagine my football career ending the way it did. And you want to know something funny? As soon as I stepped back into the locker room, the same coaches who undervalued and underappreciated me asked me, "Why in the hell did you quit? You were the best running back we had." At that moment, I wanted to unleash a fury of rage, but the damage had already been done. They took my love and passion for the game away from me. They snatched my joy and I hated them. I hated the town of Jackson, the people in it, and what they stood for. I hated how they treated young boys and girls who looked just like me. And unfortunately, I carried that hate with me for quite some time. But I still held onto my dream. I knew that I had the skills to play at the next level. But upon graduating from high school, I chose to attend Radford University, which didn't have a football program. So you better believe I blamed Jackson Memorial High School for that. Because if I had gone to high school anywhere else, or if they paid any attention to talent, I would have most certainly been playing college football.

Throughout my college years, I resented the town of Jackson. I was bitter. I wasn't supposed to be at a school with no football program. Even so, my dreams and aspirations never left. Once I graduated from Radford after four years, I decided to pursue my Master's in sport management from West Virginia University. In my mind, I saw this as an opportunity to further my education and to get one last shot at playing college football. But I knew that I was far behind since it had been four years since I last played an organized game. So I decided to train. Luckily, I had a close friend from my Pop Warner days who was a Division I football player at Elon University.

His parents avoided the wrath of Jackson public schools and decided to enroll him in a private institution. And even though he wasn't his team's star player, he still was granted the opportunity to play Division I football. So for the duration of the summer, we would go to the field to train and work on the skills he knew I would need to have to compete with the big boys.

After months and months of vigorous training, preparation, and workouts, it was time to put my skills to the test. I had arrived at WVU in late August, around the same time the football team held their annual walk-on tryouts. I completed all the necessary paperwork to become eligible and was ready to make a name for myself and make Jackson Memorial regret not giving me a chance. The tryout only lasted about a half-hour, but based on my performance, I was confident that I would be getting a call back from one of the coaches. At the conclusion of the workout, the coaching staff informed us (about 50 players) that if they wanted to bring us back, that we would receive an email by the end of the day. There was no doubt in my mind that I was going to be one of those people. But the day came and the day went. And I did not receive an email. I was devastated. All that hard work I had put in was for nothing and immediately, I went back to blaming Jackson. The first thing I told myself was that I shouldn't even be in this position because I should have already been playing college football for another school. Then, I told myself that the reason I didn't make the team was that I was away from the game and far behind the competition because of Jackson.

Years later, I was still bitter. But then I came to a realization. All of that hate and resentment wasn't going to get me anywhere. Those coaches probably didn't think about me anymore. Heck, why should they? It had been years since I last saw them, but the agony was all too familiar. I couldn't continue like this and I knew that I had to forgive them and if I didn't, I would carry that pain with me for the rest of my life. Sure, they may have ruined my chances of playing college football and perhaps professionally, but I wasn't going to let that become the story of my life. I needed to move on. I realized that blaming others for my failures wasn't going to get me anywhere and that I was the only one responsible for the outcomes of my life. Moreover, holding onto that grudge was only negatively impacting me and my mental health. I couldn't allow the past to affect me any longer. I had to forgive those coaches who overlooked me. I had to release those feelings of resentment towards the town in which I grew up.

Once I did, a tremendous weight was lifted off my shoulders. I was free from the pain and able to move forward. You see, there are many personal benefits of incorporating forgiveness into your life, such as a sharper mind and a freer spirit. It isn't easy, but it is necessary if you wish to heal and free yourself from past burdens. Whether or not other people deserve your forgiveness is not the question. After all, the act of forgiving is not for them, but it is for you. You deserve peace.

Give Thanks Each And Every Waking Morning

God didn't have to wake you up today – but he did, and for that, you should be grateful. As you may know, tomorrow is not promised to any man, woman, boy, or girl. We are living in a time where people are being taken from this Earth no matter how young or how old. And for many, 2020 has been the year of the unimaginable and the insufferable. But yet, you are here. You are living and breathing. No matter how many times life has knocked you down, you always seem to get right back on your feet. Despite all that has happened and is happening, you are alive. Therefore, you should always start your day with an overwhelming acknowledgment and appreciation for the state of being alive!

Each new day is a gift even if it may not necessarily feel like it at times. But the truth of the matter is that if you woke up this morning, you're extremely blessed. So it would behoove you to express a bit of gratitude for the opportunity to encounter new life and new experiences when many could not. Furthermore, the tone you set for yourself from the very moment you open your eyes can significantly influence how the remainder of your day will go. Giving thanks and expressing gratitude at the beginning of your day is one of the best, most effective ways to live a freer, more fulfilling life. Even when you don't feel like getting out of bed or if you're super exhausted and have to get up for work or school (or whatever responsibilities you may have), still give thanks! Showing appreciation for the ability to get up and fulfill your daily duties can elevate and empower you in a way like no other. I've made it a habit to try to do this every single morning.

Now, I don't tend to get much sleep because I am usually up late watching videos on YouTube or something silly on Netflix or Hulu. So more often than not, when I wake up in the morning, I'm still sleepy (I know some of you can relate to this!). Sure, there are times when I don't feel like getting out of the bed or even move! Yet, I still make it a priority to express gratitude for the new day and to just say, "thank you." I'll usually say something short like, "Thank you God for allowing me to wake up and FEEL tired" or "Thank you for giving me the ability and opportunity to experience a new day and new feelings because a lot of people didn't get to today." That's it. It's really that simple. This will help you to maintain a positive attitude not only in the morning but throughout your day, as well. And as unusual as that may sound, I promise those brief moments of dialogue can work wonders.

When you start your day with a grateful mind and spirit, you feel unstoppable. Nothing can stand in your way because this day, today, is your day.

Now, I'm not saying that your day will be perfect because a perfect day is rare to come by. However, I am saying that once you get into the habit of starting your day by showing thanks and expressing gratitude, it will become easier for you to conquer the challenges that life presents on a daily basis. While we cannot control much of what happens in our lives, one thing we can control is our approach. The unfortunate reality is that a lot of people didn't have the opportunity to get up today and encounter new life experiences, but you did. So, make it a priority to give thanks each and every waking morning, for it is a blessing and could all be taken away in the blink of an eye.

Hold Yourself Accountable For Your Actions

There is no shame in admitting when you are wrong because none of us are perfect and never will be. However, many people refuse to acknowledge when they've made a mistake and for many reasons. For some, it could be as simple as wanting to uphold and protect their ego and self-image. They don't want to be seen as weak or as a contradiction to their character or values. For others, assuming responsibility for their actions is just something they've never fully been accustomed to doing. After all, we will make mistakes, but it's how we reflect on these moments and transform our behavior as a result in which is significant. Now to be clear, holding yourself accountable does not always mean it necessarily has to be a public display. While it may be meaningful in some cases to serve as an example to others, taking a strict mental note can be just as effective. A simple, "I need to do better" can go a long way. Nevertheless, the most important thing is that when you make a mistake, you own up to it. I guarantee that doing so will produce much more favorable results rather than trying to evade responsibility for your wrongdoings.

Surely, there are going to be times when you'll slip up and experience errors in decision-making in regard to what you say and do. You won't always make the right choices and that's okay. I sure as hell haven't. This does not mean that you are a bad person but you must become capable of acknowledging your faults and assuming responsibility for your actions. You see, I have no problem with holding myself accountable because I already know that I'm going to make mistakes. I'm fully aware that

I won't always make the right decisions, therefore I'm prepared to take responsibility for my actions when things go wrong. Now I'm not just out here screwing around and acting a fool because I know mistakes are bound to happen. Trust me! I try to avoid problematic situations as much as possible. But the most important thing is that when I do mess up, I don't panic. There's no need because what's done in that moment is done. The only thing that you can do is own up to your actions, learn from them, and apply changed behavior. Yes, we're all going to slip up sometimes, but what matters most is how you choose to respond. You can either take responsibility for your actions or avoid owning up to them. It's kind of like the fight-or-flight response. Are you going to run when things get messy or are you going to stand tall and take it? The choice is entirely yours, but I can assure you that avoiding your problems now will only create more problems in the future.

On the other hand, holding yourself accountable now will keep you disciplined and motivate you to make better choices. Plus, people will respect you more if you do! While you can't take back what was said or done in a particular moment, holding yourself accountable provides direction as well as an assessment of which parts of yourself require improvement. Doing so exemplifies a certain level of maturity – which, unfortunately, some people will never attain. Self-accountability is the driving force that keeps us functioning as honest, ethical human beings in a society filled with distrust and uncertainty. It is an exceptional mindset that can substantially elevate your way of life by allowing you to evaluate and reflect on how you think, act, and communicate with yourself and others. Additionally, when you demonstrate self-accountability, you also encourage others to hold themselves accountable for their actions. Becoming a leader in this aspect will foster an environment where people are honest, trustworthy, and sincere. It will help people to understand that it's perfectly okay to make a mistake and own up to it. So, become comfortable with holding yourself accountable. It won't make you any less of a man or a woman by doing so. After all, our failures and missteps play a significant role in shaping and molding us into the unique individuals that we are today. And remember, a mistake only remains a mistake if you fail to learn from it!

Lead By Example

Be the change you wish to see in the world. When you lead by example, you motivate others to adhere to your set of behaviors, habits, and lifestyles. So let me just start by saying this – there is ALWAYS someone who is watching you. We are living in a society where we are constantly criticized, analyzed, and evaluated, so we must keep this in mind and act accordingly. The decisions you make in regard to what you do and say not only affect you, but also those around you. While it's very possible to lead by example in a negative way, I want to stress the importance of leading by example in a way that is beneficial to society. Again, there is always someone who is watching you. And even if someone is not always physically watching you, there is invariably someone who looks up to you.

Does anybody come to mind? Perhaps a younger brother or sister, a little cousin, or maybe someone in the neighborhood who wants to be just like you. Whoever it may be, just know that they are watching. That's why you must remind yourself that what you do does not only affect you, your actions affect your family, close friends, and those who look up to you, too. For instance, if your little brother sees you stealing money from your mother's purse, he'll most likely think that there's nothing wrong with this behavior and that this act is perfectly normal. Odds are he'll probably even try snatching a little something for himself the next time the opportunity presents itself because he wants to be just like you. However, if you ask your mother for some money when you need it instead of digging in her purse, this too will catch the eye of your little brother and encourage him to do the same. That's just a small illustration of how leading by example negatively and positively can have significantly contrasting results.

However, before you can become a leader for others, you must first lead yourself. You must commit to change and step into the role of responsibility. You must put your childish ways behind you and aspire to be better than yesterday. Being a leader in today's society takes a great amount of courage. Even so, you can make a tremendous impact simply by being a "doer." A "doer" is somebody who does just that. They do. They lead. But once you assume the position as a leader for yourself and others, you must remember to lead with your actions as well as your words. If what you say and what you do are not in sync, your effectiveness as a true leader will surely diminish. As we take a look back in history, we see many cases of those who chose to lead by example.

Dr. Martin Luther King Jr. was one of those people. Now I don't need to get into a deep context of who he was or what he was about because you are all probably very familiar with this great, historic figure. But notice that whenever Dr. King spoke, he also put those words into action. Dr. King was a doer. We saw that through his numerous speeches, marches, boycotts, and so on. This was a prime example of a man who decided to lead and do so in a way that would impact millions of people for generations to come.

Today, we can reference such figures as Colin Kaepernick. I don't think that I can come up with a better model of someone who leads by example. This man literally sacrificed his entire career because he decided to be a leader and speak up for what he strongly believed, knowing his expressions were very unpopular amongst many at the time. But Kaepernick didn't mind. He used his platform in a way that would transcend to a greater amount of people so that his message could be heard. He knew that he had an opportunity to reach society as a whole simply because of his status and his fame. He was a voice for the voiceless! Unfortunately, his act of bravery cost him his career. But I challenge you to be like Colin Kaepernick.

Of course, I don't expect you to go to the lengths that he did, but you get my point. Be a voice for the voiceless. Stand up for what you believe in even if it isn't popular amongst your peers. Utilize your abilities and the platform that God gave you to inspire others and commit to change. Don't simply talk the talk. Walk the walk! If you can successfully implement these specific elements of leadership into your life, then other people will become motivated and encouraged to mirror your behavior. However, it becomes critical that you remain consistent in how you conduct yourself in order to set clear expectations of what is acceptable and what is not. So remember, lead by example, but do so in a positive manner. Be kind and respect others. Listen to people and be mindful of what you say. Put in the work. Don't always take the easy road. Aspire to be better than you were yesterday each and every day. Be a doer. Set the standard and expectations for those around you. Lead by example, and others will have no choice but to observe, reflect, and react.

With that said, if you can inspire one, you can inspire many. But keep in mind that you are not perfect and you never will be. You will continue to make mistakes and fall short, but as long as you persist and put in the conscious effort to be the change you wish to see, you can surely make a difference in the world.

Less Opinion, More Perspective

These wise words were spoken by one of my biggest personal inspirations – Bay Area rapper and author Brandon McCartney, aka Lil B. And although this statement is of few words, it sure does present great significance. But what does it exactly mean? Essentially, the message this bit of information is conveying is to become more accepting and open-minded towards the opinions and opposing viewpoints of others. Many times, the opinions we formulate in our minds originate from our egos. Meaning, when we develop these judgments, we typically do so in a way that complements and reinforces our own beliefs, values, and views. While this isn't anything unusual or uncommon, it does often interfere with our ability to understand and learn from other people. Especially those who aren't quite like you and those who occupy a different set of values than your own.

The fact of the matter is that humans were placed on this Earth to help one another. By taking just a brief moment to understand other people and opposing opinions, we can benefit ourselves by acquiring valuable information, expanding our minds, and applying what we've learned to our everyday lives. This doesn't mean that we always have to agree with one another, but we should at least take the time to listen. Picture this: You and a friend decide that you want to take a road trip. Let's just say that the two of you plan to drive from New York to Florida. That's quite the trip – 17 hours to be exact. But this isn't the first time you've made this voyage because you have family who lives in Florida and once a year, you would drive down by yourself to visit.

So, as you and your friend are ready to depart and embark on the long journey ahead, you check your GPS and, just as you expected, 17 hours. Your friend (who also happens to be a geography major) looks over and verifies the time. But right before the two of you take off, your friend pulls out a map and says, "I know a way we can take that will cut two hours off of our trip. We'll have to take some back roads along the way, but I'm certain that we can save about two hours." As they're explaining this to you, they also identify many different points and lines throughout the map, which makes absolutely zero sense to you.

One thing you do know, though, is that you've made this trip countless times, much more than your friend has, and it always takes the same time. So because of what you already know, you say, "I appreciate you trying to help, but I just don't think we can take that risk. We can take the way I usually go, and we'll be there in 17 hours" (keep in mind, you're not the geography major here). But anyway, the two of you agree. However, before you can even make it twenty minutes down the road, your friend turns to you, pleading that you take their advice and travel the alternative route, which would cut two hours off the trip. You are skeptical, but because of their geographical background, you give them the benefit of the doubt and follow their lead. You take a few back roads and finally arrive in Florida – 15 hours later. "Less opinion, more perspective."

My point is that we don't have all the answers! Yet sometimes we will allow our ego or pride get in the way of reaching a goal or seeking a solution. Believe it or not, you don't have all the answers. But there is always someone out there who knows something you don't – and vice versa. Think about it, life would be boring if you had it all figured out every step of the way. Oftentimes, you will need to explore beyond your personal chamber of knowledge to acquire what you desire. That is the way God intended it to be and a strong indication that every now and then, we are the very ones who block our blessings.

I don't want you to get confused and think as if you need to reach out to somebody for another perspective every time you become faced with a problem or an issue. It's okay to figure things out on your own. You may already have the answers to a particular problem or a specific situation, which is fine. But that doesn't mean that you should exclude the opinions and ideas of other people because what they possibly can bring to the table just might elevate your experience even more. Ultimately, what we know is not of the utmost importance. Rather, it is what someone else can teach us that holds true value. Therefore, you only hurt yourself when you choose to be closed-minded. There are many different types of people throughout the world, with many different outlooks and contrasting views. So, take the time to listen to others. Learn from one another. You will be surprised as to what they might be able to teach you.

Look To Serve Rather Than To Be Served

Instead of being somebody who always relies on other people, be somebody who other people can always rely on. You will often find more joy in what you can do for others rather than what you can do for yourself. To be clear, there is nothing wrong with being served, but one should not make a living of it. You may be asking yourself, what does it mean to serve?

To serve can mean a variety of things, such as teaching somebody how to do something, lending a helping hand when in need, or simply offering guidance to someone who may be struggling. The list is endless. Essentially, to serve is to be of assistance, and while you can, you should strive to be of assistance more than you need to be assisted. Even the Lord Jesus Christ himself said, "It is more blessed to give than to receive." After all, humans were placed on this Earth to help one another, so you never know the impact that a simple act of kindness can have on another individual.

It took me a while to come to this realization. Growing up, I was extremely blessed. I was fortunate enough to be raised in a household with two loving parents who would risk it all for me, my older sister, and my twin brother. They would always try to find things to do for us to keep us satisfied. That's just the type of parents they were, and still are, to this day. But the older I got, the more I realized something. My parents dedicated their entire lives serving us. Even at times when we didn't ask for anything, they provided. And while it felt good to have somebody who was constantly in your corner, I felt as if it was my time to step up. After all, I wasn't getting any younger, and I knew I had to approach manhood sooner or later. So, I did. I told myself that I was going to start to serve my parents more and expect less from them. I'm not talking about helping around with the little things such as washing the dishes or taking out the trash (even though my parents did appreciate that), but I wanted to serve them in a way that would take some pressure off their shoulders and alleviate some stress they may have had. My mission was to look to serve rather than to be served.

I started doing things around the house such as cleaning, cooking dinner for the family, and checking on my nana (may her soul rest in peace) so that my mother didn't have to all the time. I even started scheduling my own doctors and dentist appointments! (Yes, I know that seems like a simple task, but in our household, this was a major accomplishment). My point is, whatever the chore, I wanted to be of assistance and not the assisted. And not only was I accomplishing my goal, but I also felt good doing it. It felt good to put a smile on my parent's faces. It felt good to see them be able to relax for a bit because they weren't so overwhelmed with responsibilities. And above all, it just felt good to do something for somebody else. I had found more joy in giving back to my parents than any other thing they had ever given me.

Try applying this to your everyday life. Search for ways you can help others more than you need others. Be there for someone. You might not only make somebody's day, but you'll feel good while doing it. And remember, to serve does not necessarily require physical labor. You can volunteer your time to an elder, perhaps a grandparent. You could offer words of wisdom or sound advice to someone younger than you, such as a sibling. Try it, and you will be shocked to see the impact you can have on somebody else. Additionally, simply lending a helping hand helps to keep us in touch with reality by understanding the struggles of others.

Sometimes, we allow ourselves to become so fascinated by the false perception of the glorified lives of stars and celebrities that we tend to forget that it's okay to struggle and that most people do. So, look for ways to be of assistance. Help somebody in need. Lend a helping hand. Look to serve rather than to be served. You will not only benefit the other person, but you will feel better about yourself too.

Love Yourself First

At the end of the day, you're all you got. Sometimes we get so caught up in caring for and tending to the needs of others that we forget to take care of the most important person – you. While it's all well and good to do for other people, you must not become so absorbed with their lives that you begin to neglect your own wants and needs. But what does it really mean to love yourself first? And why is it so imperative?

To begin, loving yourself first means that you are completely confident in your own skin regardless of what anyone thinks or says about you. It is accepting you for who you are and always maintaining a positive self-image. It is learning to accept your flaws and imperfections, but at the same time, committing to constant improvement. This can be extremely difficult to do, especially if you're like me, and you're your own worst critic. But one must understand that you are not perfect, so you must not expect perfection. Let go of your past mistakes, move forward, and fully embrace your journey!

But loving yourself first goes far beyond just that. When you love yourself wholly, you begin to treat yourself as you would anyone else that you love. Just how it takes time, patience, and effort to love someone else, you must reciprocate that same energy towards you. Just how you show compassion towards other people and their feelings, you must show yourself compassion. When you love yourself first, you silence the voices in your head that always seem to focus on the negative. You become much less self-critical by allowing yourself to make mistakes, and more importantly, realizing that it's not the end of the world when you do. Additionally, you make sacrifices and choices that will benefit you now and in the future because you understand that your health and wellness are an essential part of your success and longevity.

Loving yourself first isn't easy, but it is necessary if you wish to enhance the overall quality of your life. And that doesn't mean that you are self-absorbed or a narcissist. It simply means that you are deeply connected with yourself and profoundly in tune with your needs and desires. Always remember that you are your top priority, but not your only priority. It becomes nearly impossible to love another being until you first learn to love yourself. Think about it – how can you know how to love somebody else if you don't know how to love yourself? How can you fully accommodate and satisfy the needs of others when you can't even satisfy yourself? The answer is simple – you can't. You may think that you can, but you're only fooling yourself. Once you truly learn to love yourself first, then you'll be able to take the love that's within and spread it throughout the world. So, remember, love yourself first, so that you can love other people – the right way. But don't become so self-centered that you lose sight of what's really important and forget about those who love and care for you the most. Love yourself first so that you may get the most out of life!

Make Every Moment Count

Because truthfully, you never know when it's going to be your last. Life is exceedingly short, so it's essential that you make the most out of every situation and maximize your opportunities. When you make moments count, you understand that your time is precious and invaluable. Therefore, you don't just sit around and let it pass you by. Instead, you get up, get on your feet, and get to the bag. You set goals for yourself and then work towards accomplishing them. You fully commit yourself to life's experiences and put forth your best effort in everything that you do. You make time for who and what you want, and you don't put off until tomorrow what you can do today. Essentially, when you make moments count, you create meaningful memories that could last a lifetime. But, perhaps the most crucial aspect of making every moment count is the ability to appreciate the present moment.

Many times, we allow ourselves to get caught up in our thoughts and in our minds, which can often be self-destructive. We become so stuck worrying about our past and contemplating our future that we forget to live in the present. This is probably one of my worst habits, and I know some of you can relate. But for whatever reason, it seems as if I'm always worrying about my future. And sometimes, I get so caught up in my head that I distract myself from what's happening right in front of me. But still, I worry. I worry about whether or not all the work I'm putting in for school will eventually lead to a successful career. I worry about the possibility of being a failure and potentially disappointing my family. I worry and wonder if there really are better days ahead. Those are just a few of my biggest worries, but I am trying to minimize them altogether. Because if there's one thing I learned in life, it's that worrying about the future gets you nowhere. When you worry about the future, it actually passes you right by. You create your future by what you do in the present. So when you become stuck worrying about the future, you lose valuable time that you could have spent building your future. And unfortunately, once that time has passed, you can't get it back.

I think the main reason why I worry so much about the future is that I'm fearful that I won't be successful. I'm afraid that I won't amount to anything and that I'll let all my loved ones down. But I have to continually remind myself that I can't get caught up in my thoughts and become worried about what may happen. Because truth is, nobody knows what's going to happen. None of us can predict the future. So instead of worrying about the future, let's work towards it by doing what we can do today. My plea to you is this: Destroy the destructive habit of procrastination and start pursuing your ambitions. Don't count the days, but make the days count. Cherish the time you have with people because one day, these moments will be nothing but memories. And above all, live in the present and make every moment matter because it could all come to an end in an instant.

Minimize Your Worries

Whatever is meant for you will always find its way. While it's impossible to eliminate our worries entirely, there are countless ways we can reduce our worries and reach a sustained state of serenity. I think I can speak for a lot of people when I say that worry is something that is on my mind often. And while it's perfectly normal to worry in some cases, constant worry can surely take a tremendous toll on your overall health and well-being.

Worries come in all different sorts, sizes, and significances, so it becomes paramount that you can comprehend how to manage these worries and how to differentiate between those that are legitimate and those that are not. Because truthfully, sometimes we worry about things we have no business worrying about. And that just adds unnecessary stress and anxiety to our already complicated lives. However, if you are someone who commonly has difficulty distinguishing their worries, try getting acquainted with The Serenity Prayer, penned by the late American theologian Reinhold Niebuhr. This prayer changed my life, and it could change yours, too. For those who are not yet acquainted, it reads as follows: "God, grant me the serenity to accept the things I cannot change, courage to change the things I can, and wisdom to know the difference." Familiarizing myself with this particular passage and applying it to my everyday life has allowed me to minimize my worries by focusing only on the things that are in my control.

Which brings me to my next point – you must not direct your worries towards situations that are out of your control. You'll just wind up wasting time and energy. I had to learn this the hard way. But after a few times, I realized it was pointless to worry about the things in which I had no control. Because at the end of the day, you just can't prevent certain things from happening in life. But you can prepare. Let me give a quick example, which I'm sure many of you can attest to. You're in school, and you have a huge exam that's coming up. You barely know any of the material, but studying's no fun, so you decide to pass on that. You walk into the classroom the day of the exam, surprisingly confident and carefree. The instructor hands you the exam, you start to look through it, and then it hits you. You don't know a damn thing on this exam. You go from confident and carefree to clueless and crying. Ok, maybe you're not full-blown crying, but the worry is starting to sink in. Anyway, you finish the test, turn it in, and almost immediately, it becomes the only thing that consumes your mind until you find out how you did.

Don't you think this story could've gone much differently if you had just decided to study in the first place? If you had just chosen to prepare for the exam when you first heard about it, you would've easily had more than enough time to review and digest all the material beforehand. So, instead of being clueless, crying, and imprisoning yourself in a constant state of worry, you can remain confident and carefree because you decided to do what you had to do.

The lesson of that short story is this: By directing our focus only to the things we can control, we can vastly reduce our worries by knowing that whatever happens, we did our part, and there's nothing more that we could've said or done to prevent or change that particular outcome. So, the next time you start to worry about something, ask yourself, "Can I do anything about the situation?" If the answer is no, then there's no need to worry. But if the answer is yes, well, do what you have to do and let the chips fall where they may. We cannot evade our worries entirely, but we can become capable of managing which ones we allow to affect us. It's not easy to do at first, but as you know, mastering any skill requires discipline and commitment.

To summarize, less worry equals less stress and less anxiety, which we all could use. Continue to control the things you can control, and everything will be just fine.

Never Let The Words Or Actions Of Someone Else Take You Out Of Your Character

The key to a happy life is to stay true to yourself at all times and never let someone persuade you to be someone or something you are not. Your character is the set of traits, morals, and values in which you possess that helps distinguish you from others. But believe it or not, your character and individuality are challenged regularly, often by those closest to you.

There are many external factors that can influence a person's character, such as peer-pressure, surroundings, and the desire to fit in or belong to a particular group. Yet, you must stay persistent and unwavering amidst these circumstances and remain true to yourself. Because the moment you allow the words or actions of another person to take you out of your character, they have control over you. Here's a quick example. You and a long-time buddy both attend a local community college. You've always been an exceptional 4.0 student, but to cut down on the cost of tuition, you decide to start at community college. After you complete your courses, you plan to transfer to a prestigious university to further your education. Your buddy, on the other hand, is only enrolled in the community college because he didn't have any immediate plans and his parents demanded that he go to school. Despite your academic differences, the two of you are very close and even share one of the same classes.

One day, you decide to carpool to that class with your friend. You arrive at the college, but before you can even get out of the car, your friend pulls out a bottle of liquor and chugs it for about five seconds before turning to you. "Well, don't be a wuss," they eagerly say. But you have never done anything like this before because you have always been fully committed to your academics. Besides, your goals and ambitions are much more important than a bottle of liquor. You contemplate the situation for a second and then say to yourself, "one time won't hurt." So your friend hands you the bottle and the next thing you know, the two of you are stumbling up the stairs walking to class. You wanted to appease your friend so much that not only are you drunk in class, but you've completely forgotten about the homework assignment that was due. You are clearly in a bad position, all because you allowed one person to take you out of your character.

But let's take it a step further. Remember your dreams and aspirations of transferring to a prestigious university? Well, unfortunately, those dreams went down the drain that day you decided to drink. Because now, you and your "friend" have made it a ritual to chug a bottle of liquor every day before class. As a result, you start showing up late to class, your grades start to slip, and your motivation is completely lost. As time goes on, you have transformed from this star student to a community college dropout. I know this scenario is a bit extreme, but I promise you it's possible. My point is that the moment you allow someone else to take you out of your character is the moment you relinquish the title of commander of your life.

Now let me give you a short story that might be a bit more relatable. A short time ago, I was in a relationship with an extraordinary woman. We met in college, and almost instantly, I knew that she was different. We immediately clicked and shared many things in common. But there was one huge difference. She had a short-temper. I, on the other hand, was someone who had never been easily annoyed or angered, so it was rare for me to yell, shout, or raise my voice, even in intense situations. This significant dissimilarity proved to be an initial concern, but I figured it was something that would eventually resolve itself. Besides, I was head over heels for this woman, and I firmly believed that we could make this relationship work, regardless of our differences.

We made it work for quite some time. However during this time, I began to notice that my behaviors were starting to change. As my partner remained short-tempered, I became short-tempered. I became irritable, especially when dealing with the conflicts that we faced in our relationship. Instead of handling our problems in my calm, cool, and usual way, I started to adapt to my partner's way of resolving issues, which involved a lot of arguing and shouting. Things I typically wouldn't do. Without a doubt, I was acting out of character. Now, don't get it twisted – I'm not blaming her for responding the way that I did because, ultimately, those were my decisions. Yet, I was so into this person that I allowed myself to conform to their hurtful habits, and I started to lose sight of who I was. Our relationship had started great, but it soon turned toxic, and once it became unhealthy, there was no turning back. I had become stuck in my newfound ways. It seemed as if I was always arguing and yelling, and truthfully, I was tired of it. That wasn't me. Not only was I hurting myself by getting out of character, but I was hurting the relationship as a whole. Ultimately, we decided to go our separate ways and I think that was the best option going forward for us both.

You may have had similar experiences during your life, whether it was with a partner or perhaps with a friend. If this happens to be the case, I'm sure you're aware of how easy it can be for someone to take you out of your character or make you act a certain way, especially if you care deeply about that person. Even so, you must remind yourself of who you are and what you stand for. Once you begin to detect a shift in your behaviors as a response to these individuals, it is time for you to reflect on the situation, gather your thoughts and emotions, and acknowledge your true self. Sometimes, even the best option is to remove yourself from that relationship altogether because, eventually, it becomes destructive to everyone involved. But if there's one piece of advice I would like for you to take from this message, it is this: Just be you. Live authentically and never let the words or actions of someone else take you out of your character. You are the commander of your life!

Practice Patience

You may have heard the phrase "patience is a virtue," which is true. However, patience is also a skill that one must persistently train to develop. We are living in a time where it seems as if more and more people are rushing through life. There's constant pressure from society and external sources to experience as much as we can as fast as we can. If we don't, we may feel as if we're missing out on something. But, I'm here to tell you that life is not a race or a competition. Inevitably, there will be times during your life when you will experience delays, disappointment, and setbacks. Even so, you cannot let these troubles discourage or deter you because, ultimately, they will be a part of your life.

Practicing patience provides a solution to these problems by allowing you to understand that most good things take time. Meaning, we can't always expect rapid results or get frustrated when working towards a task. It's pivotal that you remain patient and persistent. For example, let's say that you recently acquired a gym membership, and your goal is to lose twenty pounds. You know that this journey will take a ton of discipline and commitment, but you're up for the challenge. You arrange your schedule so that you have enough time to go to the gym five times a week for one hour. Day 1 arrives, and you're determined to shed those pounds. You get to the gym, and you do all these different types of cardio exercises until your sweat becomes so intense that it looks like you just jumped into a pool. You implement that same routine for the first week, along with adjusting your diet at home. That weight is coming off!

At the end of Week 1, you decide to weigh yourself, anticipating that you have lost at least a couple of pounds. But to your dismay, you've only lost one pound. Really, one pound? Was this what all that hard work and healthy dieting were going to get you, one pound? Now, you have one of two options. Are you going to give up or keep going? You're highly disappointed in your results after the first week, but you know that you can't quit now, and you also know that most good things take time. So, you persist. You become patient with the process. And while the process took longer than you had hoped, here you are, two months later, and twenty pounds down.

You see, when you practice patience, you open up the door for growth and opportunity. So many times, we slam that door shut because we are not willing to put in the time, effort, and persistence needed to endure and overcome our hardships. By integrating a little patience into our lives, we can experience so much more and evolve into the better versions of ourselves we wish to become. Furthermore, while it's essential to exercise patience within ourselves, it's also imperative that we practice it with other people. Practicing patience with family, friends, and peers will immensely improve our relationships by allowing us to be more compassionate and understanding towards others.

There have been plenty of times when your patience was put to the test when dealing with other people. Maybe you were stuck waiting on somebody to go somewhere, but they were taking entirely too long to get ready. Or, maybe you're in the checkout line at the store and the person in front of you decides that they want to take their sweet time with their transaction. Or perhaps, everyone's personal favorite, you are on the road, but you're stuck in traffic. These are all common external factors that test our patience daily, but it's how you respond to these events in which is critical.

While we cannot control much of what goes on around us, the one thing we can control is our reactions. Practicing patience provides perspective by helping us learn and understand how others may think or feel. It also allows us to take a step back, gather our emotions, and analyze a situation before we act. As a result, we become more approachable and enjoyable to be around. Additionally, the sooner you master patience, the sooner you will achieve sustained success in all aspects of your life. Patience reminds us that most good things take time and that all good things come to those who wait. After all, Rome wasn't built in a day. My friend, life is short, but that doesn't mean it needs to be rushed. Take your time and always remain patient and persistent. Once you do that, everything else will fall into place.

Push Through The Tough Times

Your future self will thank you. As my mother would always say to me, "nothing good comes easy." And the more life I experience, the more I can attest this to be 100% true. Nothing good comes easy, and if it comes easy, then it's probably not worth having. Life, as we know it, is filled with adversity. We are all destined to face numerous challenges and obstacles over the course of our lives. Unfortunately, that's just the way it is, and we can't escape it. But, we do have a choice. And it might be the most important choice you ever make. You can choose to confront and conquer these challenges or allow them to repeatedly break you down to the point where you become physically and mentally defeated. There is a famous quote by the author Joshua J. Marine that reads, "Challenges are what make life interesting, and overcoming them is what makes life meaningful." Now, the good thing is, most of the struggles and hardships you are bound to endure are often temporary. And while these times may seem unbearable and never-ending, I can assure you that tough times don't last forever.

Take a moment to think about a time where you faced adversity. Maybe you had to pass a difficult class in order to graduate. Perhaps you experienced a painful, heart-wrenching breakup. Or maybe, you had to deal with a devastating loss of a loved one. Now, I want you to think about how you confronted and overcame those obstacles and how it made you feel. Isn't it remarkable just to be able to sit back and think about how far you've come, despite your doubts? To face adversity, go through it, and come out the other side unscathed, is truly an amazing feeling. You see, the only way to overcome adversity is to go through it. You must not hide or shy away from it. Instead, embrace each adversity as an opportunity. Use them as opportunities for personal growth and development and to work on your weaknesses.

I want to tell you about a time when I faced extreme adversity and how I overcame it. I was a sophomore at Radford University, and I had just started a new role as a Resident Assistant for the college's largest on-campus residence hall. This particular building housed nearly 1,000 freshmen and underclassmen, so you can only imagine the type of stuff that went on in there. Now I didn't necessarily want to be an RA, but the tuition rates for out-of-state students were through the roof. I knew I had to do something to substantially cut down that cost if I wanted to stay at that school. So I signed up for the RA interviews, and when it was all said and done, I got the position. The following semester, I was assigned as the RA on the 4th floor A-wing of this 13-story dorm. Now

I'm in a good spot financially. My tuition is reduced, my room and board and meal plan are covered, and the best perk of them all (well, to me, at least) is that I had an entire room to myself. But I wasn't your typical RA, and I think any of my residents could testify to that. I didn't write anybody up, and I didn't bust anybody for alcohol. I went out to parties with my residents, and I even hosted a few of my own in my room. Anything we weren't supposed to do as RA's, I probably did.

Looking back on it now, I was probably the worst RA in the history of RA's, but as long as I wasn't getting caught, I was okay with it. Besides, these were all grown-ass adults, and I was not going to spend my free time babysitting. To my surprise, I make it past the first semester and even a couple of months into the second. Boy, was I finessing. But little did I know, my life was about to take a drastic turn. It's a normal day in March, and per usual, I'm up to no good. I left one of my classes early so I could smoke and grab some food, which wasn't anything out of the ordinary for me. But this day was anything but that. After getting my food, I returned to the room to kick it and watch TV. Then suddenly, I hear a loud pounding at the door. So I head towards the door, open it slowly, and when I do, immediately, I know I'm in trouble. Have you ever had that feeling? When you can just look at somebody and sense that you are in trouble? I know you know that feeling. So, after giving me that "you know why I'm here" stare for a couple of seconds, the man at my door asks me (even though he already knew the answer) why my hallway reeked of marijuana. Ok, now I'm nervous. But, me being the finesser that I am, I had an answer for that. So I tell the man that the halls usually smell like marijuana because there are a lot of students who like to smoke that reside in this building (which I wasn't lying about). But even with such an impressive, on-the-spot answer as that, he doesn't seem to buy it. Which, I can't blame him for because we both knew that I knew exactly where the smell was coming from. I had just smoked, and you could see it clear as day in my eyes. Not only does this man not believe me, but he then proceeds to call campus police for further investigation.

Now I'm REALLY nervous. But I knew I had some time before they got there, so I had to act fast. I shut the door and quickly returned to my room to put away anything marijuana-related and spray the area. As I'm doing this, the man at the door, who I later found out was the fire safety inspector, patiently waited outside for the police to arrive. About five minutes later, I hear another loud banging at the door. Ok, this was it. Will the police believe my story or would they reveal the truth? I open the door as confidently and as sober as I can, and, like the fire safety inspector, they again ask me why the hallways reeked of marijuana. So, I tell them exactly what I said to the fire safety inspector. However, now I'm dealing with the police, so regardless of what I tell them, they can still search my room if they have probable cause. And you better believe they did. As I stand by my bed helplessly watching them go through my belongings, I started to think the worst.

They went through everything, and I mean everything. They threw all my clothes out of my dresser, they ravished through my desks and drawers, and they even searched the bathroom. And it was at that very moment that I had realized that I'd forgotten to take the alcohol out of the fridge. When they finally got to it, I watched them take each bottle and pour every last drop down the drain. They might as well have poured all my hopes and dreams down there, too. So after their little "raid", all they were able to find was a grinder and a few bottles of alcohol. It definitely could've been much worse.

But being that I was on-campus and in a leadership position, I was not allowed to have any of those items in my possession. To make a long story short, my boss was alerted about the situation, and I was out of a job within the next hour. Not only was I out of a job, but I only had two days to find a new place to stay for the remainder of the semester because the university would no longer finance my room and board arrangements. But I think maybe the worst thing that came from all of this was the fact that I had to face my parents and tell them the truth. That was by far the worst part because I knew that I had let them down and potentially ruined my chances of returning to Radford. And they weren't going to find another place for me to stay since I had gotten myself into this mess, so I needed to get myself out. Luckily, I had a close friend that lived in an apartment off-campus who let me move in with her until the end of the semester, and to this day, I don't know how I would've finished school if she had not been so exceptionally kind (shout-out to you, you know who you are). Those last two months of school were quite challenging, as I had to quickly adjust from having my own room to sleeping on a couch, being on-campus to taking the bus to class, and a whole lot of other things that I had taken for granted. My mother and father were extremely disappointed in me, and rightfully so. Now we had to figure out how we were going to cover my tuition and other expenses for the remainder of the semester and the following year. Oh yeah, I forgot to mention that I had just got hired to be an RA my junior year, but once I got fired, that went down the drain, too.

While my future at Radford University was in jeopardy, one thing I did know was that I was going to do everything in my power to make sure I returned in the fall. I already knew that I was going to have to acquire a decent-enough paying job to provide some financial assistance to my family. It wasn't expected of me to cover my tuition in-full, but my parents made it clear that since this was a result of my poor choices, I was going to pay (literally and figuratively). Not to mention, I had an aunt who was a professor at Radford, so when all of this had initially happened, I went to her office to let her know the mess I had gotten myself in.

She suggested to me that I take a look at working at Dish Network over the summer, as it was a popular, high-paying job for college students in the area. So, I did. Before the end of that semester, I had set up an interview, and right at the start of summer, I was employed by Dish Network as a customer service representative. I had never done anything like this before, but as I said, I was willing to do anything I had to do to stay at Radford. But mind you, this was a summer job, so I had to acquire some sort of housing. Again, lucky enough for me, the same friend who had let me crash at her crib for the rest of the semester let me stay at her spot for the summer. Of course, I had to pitch in a little for rent and utilities, but I didn't care. I was grateful to have a place to stay and to get a chance to prove to my parents that I could make this work. But I knew it wasn't going to be easy.

My new job wasn't easy, either. Honestly, it was probably one of the hardest jobs that I've ever had. Now I know you're probably thinking to yourself that talking on the phone to a bunch of Dish Network customers about their TV bill doesn't seem too challenging, but boy, let me tell you. Do you know how hard it is to explain to a customer step-by-step, line-by-line, why their bill went up a whopping $5 a month while they swear up and down that you have no idea what you're talking about? Or how about this one: informing a customer that their current television package doesn't have a specific channel they want, so they plead and beg for you to just magically add that one channel to their TV (sorry, it doesn't work like that). And that was just the beginning of it. Seems pretty ridiculous, right? Yet, I would get those types of calls all day on top of being cussed out and called everything in the book by a bunch of strangers. But, hey, this was paying the bills, so I had to push through.

To summarize, that was a long, difficult summer. I could've easily given up when times got tough, but I faced my adversity, I went through it, and I came out the other side a winner. Ultimately, by the grace of God, I was able to finish my undergraduate college career at Radford, and now I'm in my 2nd and final year of the sport management master's program at West Virginia University. If you take anything away from this piece, let it be to push through the tough times and never give up. You are capable of so much more than you think. We only have one shot at this thing we call life, so be fearless in your journey. Be relentless and unyielding when faced with life's biggest challenges. Be courageous, and don't allow your problems to become bigger than your purpose. But if you still find trouble pushing through the hard times, seek motivation through external sources such as loved ones, family members, and close friends. They can be an excellent support system and a powerful reminder that you are not alone in this journey.

We're all going to go through tough times, but we cannot allow these circumstances to alter our goals and aspirations. Ultimately, we must choose to suffer from one of two pains: the pain of discipline or the pain of regret. The choice is yours. Nothing good comes easy, so continue to persist and be patient in your struggles! And remember, tough times don't last. Tough people do.

Refrain From The Judgment Of Others

In other words, don't judge a book by its cover. The reality is, we are all judgmental in some way, shape, or form, myself included. And while it may be just a part of our human nature, I can assure you that we do not gain anything from passing judgment onto other people. Besides, it isn't our place to judge others because none of us are perfect – not today, not tomorrow, or ever. So why do we allow ourselves to critique and criticize other people without even knowing the person? Well, I'll tell you why. But first, let me just say that in most cases, our judgments derive from ignorance.

When we judge other people, we do so simply because we don't understand them or because they are somewhat different than us. And typically, when we judge others, we judge them by our own standards or what society has deemed as acceptable. We analyze the elements of a person's external appearance, such as their physique, wardrobe, and looks, and almost immediately make an assumption about who or what type of person they are. However, the major flaw with this approach is that we are only exposed to the exterior, indicating that we seldom search for what's beneath the surface of an individual. And I think that's a significant problem we have in the world today; we judge before we know.

It's easy to evaluate someone based on the type of clothes that they wear and how "fit" or well-kept they may or may not look. But until you actually take the time to get to know somebody, your judgments are nothing but assumptions. As the late, great American poet Walt Whitman once said, "Be curious, not judgmental." Additionally, when you judge by jumping to conclusions, you create an unnecessary divide between you and others. You eliminate the possibility of forming meaningful connections and establishing favorable relationships simply because of your convictions. Yet, everyone is different and unique in their own way. So instead of trying to paint false perceptions of people, get to know them, learn to accept them, and embrace their individuality. Plus, wouldn't life be boring if everybody was just like you, or if everybody dressed like you, or talked like you? Truth is, we need people who aren't like us because they can teach us things that we may not know. Also, it's important to note that if everybody was exactly the same, we'd all go insane. We must learn to love and accept people from all different cultures and backgrounds because, ultimately, our cultural diversity is what makes life fascinating.

Furthermore, sometimes we judge others based on what we may have heard about them. But if you think about it, this isn't really fair. Has this ever happened to you? Have you ever been going to meet somebody for the first time, but because of what somebody else already told you about them, you've already formulated an opinion on who or what type of person they are? I've certainly been in similar situations, and from my experience, this is one of the worst things you could do. Why? Because we are all different in someone else's eyes. What one person may think of you could be entirely the opposite of what somebody else may think.

Sometimes, you will be the villain in other people's stories, and sometimes, you will be the hero. But just because these people portray you in a different light doesn't mean that either of them is right. People must get to know you for you, not for what somebody else told them about you. I'm sure you wouldn't appreciate it if somebody judged you based upon their predetermined beliefs as a result of what somebody else told them about you. You would want that person to get to know you for themselves; therefore, you must act in the same manner.

Finally, sometimes we judge others to feel good about ourselves. We think that by pointing out the flaws and imperfections of other people, that we will pay less attention to our problems, and ultimately, feel better about ourselves. For example, if you're driving around and you see a homeless person on the side of the road, you might feel a little better about the poor decisions you've made in your life. Now, all the problems that you had before are still present, but because you see somebody else struggling far more than you, a slight burden becomes lifted off of your shoulders (for the time being). But let me tell you, just because someone appears to be worse off than you, that doesn't make you any better than them. You never know what someone may be going through or has already experienced that led them to their current situation. So be kind, and refrain from the judgment of others.

As I alluded to earlier, we have all been guilty of passing judgment in one way or another, myself included. It is a tendency we occupy that encourages discrimination, bias, and division amongst people. Thus, we must discipline ourselves to become more open-minded and not to formulate opinions of others based on our initial impressions. Above all, judging other people does not make you a better person, and it can even become exhausting if you exert excessive energy doing so. Don't limit yourself by being judgmental. Love and accept all people. Live and let live.

Stop Comparing Yourself To Others

Just be you. Life is a journey, and everyone's destination is different. So, instead of worrying about what other people may or may not be doing with their lives, focus on your path and how you can become the best version of yourself humanly possible. When we compare ourselves to others, we typically are left with feelings of envy, jealousy, and resentment. So if comparison is the thief of joy, then why do we allow ourselves to constantly get caught up in the comparison trap?

The answer is simple: self-evaluation. As humans, we have a natural need to routinely assess ourselves, our looks, our behaviors, etc. As we analyze the traits, characteristics, and material possessions of others, we utilize these elements for self-evaluation and create unrealistic expectations of what our lives should look like. But this is actually one of the worst, most dangerous things you could do because when you compare yourself to others, you dim the light of your life by stacking it up against theirs. Even so, many internal and external influences can lead you to this 'very real' comparison trap and leave you stuck in a cycle of compare and despair.

Social media is one of them. Social media platforms have become one of the biggest, most influential instigators in terms of social comparisons. Whether it's Facebook, Snapchat, Twitter, or Instagram, these social networks have played a pivotal role in pushing us towards that comparison trap. And the more time you spend scrolling through your various feeds and timelines, the more susceptible you are to becoming a victim. That is why it is paramount that you utilize these platforms purposefully, rather than in a self-destructive way. You see, people may seem to "have it all" via the content they display, however social media only shows a glimpse of reality. It isn't uncommon for others to advertise their accomplishments, which can be misleading. I say this because while many people publicize their wins, very few publicize their losses. So it makes sense for us to feel a little bit of envy towards someone when we see that they're striving. However, we have no idea what it took for that person to arrive at that position. They may have been tested with tremendous trials and tribulations along their journey. Therefore, you must remember that many will share their successes; very few will share their setbacks.

Additionally, it has been scientifically proven that the more time you spend on social media, the more likely you are to develop feelings of depression and loneliness. For instance, by analyzing what other people post, you may sense as if you're not doing enough with your life, or more commonly, fear of missing out (FOMO). FOMO is a social anxiety that originates from the belief that an exciting or interesting event may be happening elsewhere without you. But the truth is, most of the time when we experience FOMO, we're not actually missing out on anything. Remember, social media only shows a glimpse of reality, not the full picture. You don't know what occurs behind the scenes. You don't even know anything that happened that led up to the event. All you see is a photo or video that looks like people are having a good time,and that's enough to make you feel some type of way. Again, this is why it becomes highly critical that you utilize social media in a purposeful manner. Rather than allowing these constant, social comparisons to affect your mood and emotions negatively, use them as motivation to help set goals and chase your dreams.

Another faulty component of the comparison trap is that when we see something exceptional happening in someone else's life, we automatically think that it can't happen to us. For example, let's say that you and a friend apply for the same job. A couple of weeks go by, and neither of you has heard anything back yet. But one day, your friend gets a call from the job and is informed that they have been hired and can start immediately. That same day, you, too, receive a call, but with much different news. In the end, they thank you for your interest but tell you that you don't meet the criteria for the position. How could this be? You were much smarter, more charismatic, and your resume was polished. And still, they chose not to choose you. Let's take a moment to reflect. Now, it's easy to become envious of your friend who had got the job, but that wouldn't do either of you any good. You're wondering how in the world they got the job, but you, on the other hand, didn't "meet the criteria." But I want you to realize that just because someone else is accomplishing great things in their life doesn't mean you can't accomplish great things in yours.

Now let's get back to the story. After receiving the disappointing news that the job wasn't going to hire you, you start to look elsewhere for employment. As you start your search, you stumble across an ad that pays twice as much and is substantially closer to your home. Without hesitation, you apply for the job, and within days, they contact you to congratulate you on your new position with the company. So now, both you and your friend have jobs, and everything seemed to work out for the best.

You see, just because someone else is striving, that doesn't mean you can't. When you compare yourself to others, you minimize your opportunities by focusing on theirs. But you never know the journey of that individual, so it would be beneficial to eliminate social comparisons entirely. I know this can be extremely difficult, but expressing constant gratitude makes it easy to escape the comparison trap. When you express gratitude daily, you don't become worried about what other people may or may not have going on in their lives. You aren't envious or jealous of another being because you are satisfied with the things in your life, and nothing that they post or possess can make you feel any less about yourself. Once you master this, you will stop becoming a victim of the comparison trap, and you will be able to live life more freely. So, stop comparing yourself to others – it does you no good. The fact of the matter is, only you can be you, and nobody is better at being you than you. Everyone's destination is different, so learn to embrace your path and what God has specifically in store for you!

CPSIA information can be obtained
at www.ICGtesting.com
Printed in the USA
FSHW011528100221
78461FS